811.54

THE QUEEN'S DESERTION

Flint Memorial Library
147 Park St.
North Reading, MA 01864

Also by Carol Frost

THE SALT LESSON

LIAR'S DICE

THE FEARFUL CHILD

DAY OF THE BODY

CHIMERA

PURE

VENUS AND DON JUAN

LOVE AND SCORN: NEW AND SELECTED POEMS

I WILL SAY BEAUTY

THE QUEEN'S DESERTION

CAROL FROST

TriQuarterly Books

Northwestern University Press

Evanston, Illinois

TriQuarterly Books
Northwestern University Press
www.nupress.northwestern.edu

Copyright © 2006 by Carol Frost. Published 2006 by
TriQuarterly Books/Northwestern University Press.
All rights reserved.

Printed in the United States of America

10 9 8 7 6 5 4 3 2 1

ISBN 0-8101-5175-8 (cloth)
ISBN 0-8101-5176-6 (paper)

Library of Congress Cataloging-in-Publication Data

Frost, Carol, 1948–
    The queen's desertion / Carol Frost.
       p. cm.
    Poems.
    ISBN 0-8101-5175-8 (cloth : alk. paper) — ISBN
0-8101-5176-6 (pbk. : alk. paper)
    1. Loss (Psychology)—Poetry. I. Title.
PS3556.R596Q44 2006
811.54—dc22

                          2005037448

∞ The paper used in this publication meets the
minimum requirements of the American National
Standard for Information Sciences—Permanence of
Paper for Printed Library Materials, ANSI Z39.48-1992.

FOR JIM *and* "MIKE" STATHAM,

GRAHAM *and* EVELYN DUNCAN,

and MICHAEL THOMAS

⬡⬡⬡⬡⬡⬡⬡ CONTENTS

IV.   OLD PAN

○─○─○─○─○─○─○ ACKNOWLEDGMENTS

Thanks to the editors of the journals where the following poems, sometimes in earlier versions, first appeared: *Gettysburg Review* ("Drowned," "Man So Bronzed"); *Great River Review* ("Telling the Bees"); *Green Mountains Review* ("Eddy," "Voyage"); *Indiana Review* ("Apiary II"); *Kenyon Review* ("Black Point," "Dolphin," "Low Tide," "Manatee," "Songs for Two Seasons" [four sections published separately as "After Grave Illness," "Marsyas's Art," "Procedure," and "Red Pond"], "Waking"); *Massachusetts Review* ("Robinson Crusoe's Hair"); *New England Review* ("Sea Hare"); *Nightsun* ("Sandpiper"); *Ninth Letter* ("The Queen's Desertion"); *Ploughshares* ("Apiary VII," "The St. Louis Zoo"); *Poetry* ("Blue Crab," "Late," "Pelican," "The Poet's Black Drum," "Redfish," "To Fishermen,"); *Salt Hill* ("*Relación* of Cabeza de Vaca"); *Southern Review* ("Komodo"); *Subtropics* ("Lucifer in Florida"); *32 Poems* ("Boat"); *TriQuarterly* ("Clam," "Orchid," "Snake Key").

"Apiary IX" first appeared in *I Will Say Beauty* (Evanston, Ill.: Northwestern University Press, 2003); "The St. Louis Zoo" was reprinted in the seventh edition of *Contemporary American Poetry,* edited by A. Poulin Jr. and Michael Waters (New York: Houghton Mifflin, 2000); "Telling the Bees" was reprinted in the eighth edition of *Contemporary American Poetry,* edited by Michael Waters (New York: Houghton Mifflin, 2005).

THE QUEEN'S DESERTION

LUCIFER IN FLORIDA

I Lucifer, cast down from heaven's city which is the stars,
soar darkly nights across the water to islands
and their runway lights—after sunset burning petals;
sights, sorrows, all evils become the prolonged shadows
and lightning through palm trees and the ancient oaks.
. . . And ride with darkness, dark below dark, uttermost
as when the cormorant dives and the fish dies, eye-deep
in hell; the bird is I, I hide in its black shining
spread of wings raised drying afterward on a tree bough.
Nothing more onyx or gold than my dark wings.
Yet Venus rising, the off chords and tender tones
of morning birds among the almonds, small flames
of lemon flowers, phosphorus on the ocean,
all I've scorned, all this lasts whether I leave or come.
The garden fails but the earth's garden lives on
unbearable—elusive scent on scent from jasmine
mixed with brine, the smell of marshes, smells of skin
of fishermen, burned rose and a little heroic
while leviathan winds rise and darkness descends.
Sin and death stay near, black with serenity,
calm in dawn's light suggestions. If the future is
a story of pandemonium, perfection's close—
from the sea the islands at night, from the island
the sea at night with no lights rest equally, lit by
a wanderer's memory bringing dark and light to life,
luminous and far as dreams endure, charcoal and flame
in a fire, the embers of pride and pain in each breath.

I

THE QUEEN'S DESERTION

In a dark time, the eye begins to see.
Theodore Roethke

THE QUEEN'S DESERTION

Pretty to think of the mind at its end
as a metaphysician beekeeping
after the leaves have fallen at autumn's end.

Never sweeter, closer, those hours
bred from seasons. Were not the cells and stars
fruit-smelling? Where are those hours?

In the ashes of old pains and joys, in the burning
and nectar, the interstellar black garden,
the cold solstice, space inside a space once burning.

⬡–⬡–⬡–⬡–⬡–⬡

The wintriest gray shape, beauty
smoked out—no longer full of rapture and sweet lies
(see, the beekeeper's terrible blank eyes are trying

to make whoever looks see that he no longer knows
what to think, do, feel, or even what day it is, and he succeeds),
but a blunt empty box.

I see the unmarked snow,
the yawning tree, shriveled bees
on the bottom pan, and I see dead beauty.

APIARY II

Abandoned bee boxes piled on each other at meadow end . . .
Like clothing taken off,
the bees who had alighted on hat,
gloves, shirt, have flown off somewhere.
Is it so terrible to outlive the mind?
Forget this, forget that—keys, glasses,
what it was you just said, what you meant to say.
Pseudonyms. Silences:
oddball or golden and grave, a dance of signs,
sorrows passing by like shadows,
time running by like a small girl running by like a madwoman.

APIARY VII

Generous I may have been, amnesiac
I became. Autumn fattened and thinned;
I stared at the clock's senseless hands.
I let the girl in the market make change.
I looked at my lists of medicines
and the bottles on the shelf, but they
seemed separate. In the bathroom mirror
my face was suddenly antediluvian who
was I? I'd be thinking, and at the first touch
of attention, I'd forget. I cut my own hair.
I saw my mother wrapped in a mantilla
in her coffin. Why did I find my skin's
imperfections so interesting and pick off
moles? If I went to the end of the street,
would I be at the center of myself?
Insects watched me. They got in my hair.
I'd be at the opera house in Vienna.
The planes strafed the Strassenbahn.
My hands fluttered then like butterflies.
For a little while I knew—there was a door,
a split in the wall, and I was two persons,
old and young, wise and clean, sturdy and
bent, generous and dead. They were
neck on neck like winter and spring
but could do nothing for each other.
I'm leaving, I know, each said,
a flooding darkness in their eyes,
a drawing down of blinds. Afterward

my feelings were the eyes of moths.
They . . . What is the word between eyes
and too little light? I knew. I think so.
Meanings fissured. Words hollowed.
It was like the thing with bees—
I swatted in front of my face
and hated them. Then there were none.

APIARY IX

Two anthills and a late summer hive
gone to fragments.
The dirt is acrid, the wax honeyed—
so mind makes laws, dividing seasons,
scents, light and light's reflections.
I have no mother. Yes, you have a mother,
a voice said. But that is not right. Her difference—
a broken hive . . . a black bear in the bluebells
clawing the stinging air . . . something torn from her.
Still, the land soothes me—*No one may come—*:
low sun, dusk, and charred trees,
seeming first to glow as they darken, really are only darkening,
as if autumn burned.
And if I want it otherwise, O self,
there's beauty in small lies.
I say bees lick nectar after dark
and bring it to the bough of the honey tree.
Royal jelly keeps the larvae from falling
from the cells. *Broodcomb, honeycomb, bee bread—*
this is a harmless thought. Yes, once I *had* a mother.
I said to her, there is no twenty
on the clock, don't worry. I said
I will tell you the time. She said how little it takes
to finish . . . *What?*
Stupid, Orphean things swirl:
apricot flowers . . . bees circling
as many times as the distance to the nectar . . .
throbbing wings . . . buzzing . . .

then to pluck the mind from darkness
singing. Mother hears
ambient grief and, more and more,
her earlier German tongue—rhyming Schiller lines.
Where were you? I'll ask. *Wer bist du?* she'll say,
winter in voices, drifting,
snow drift, freezing, the bees dropping
to the hard pan inner darkness . . . O mother . . .

TELLING THE BEES

Will we tell the bees or bees tell us it's no sadder—another fall whoever's fall it is?
It's as if they felt for us: the sting, the swarming in the mind,
the sugar tear to probe for, or a mood to dance on air. If there were overblown
    roses
and a child spilled root beer, the bees would seem to know the difference, flying
    there,
but not care, evening too swift, autumnal. I say only listen to the hum behind the
    trees
where the white bee boxes burn in evening. Drink in the air. There's more moving
in the season's heart—seconds of snow on the steep part of the wind—
than can be stopped. The bees, small jewels, however, hand themselves over
to us. It's all right to cry, I tell myself. But it isn't sadder than it was before.

II

THE BODY HAS
TWO SEASONS

WAKING

It was dusk, the light hesitating
and a murmur in the wind, when the deer, exhausted,
turned to look at me, an arrow in its side.

Though I pity dreamers, taking a thread
and weaving it upon the loom of Self—the secret,
gaudy, wonderful new cloth—, I will tell the end of the story.

His shoulder was torn, the joint held by one sinew,
which I severed with the blade of the arrow,
so when he ran there were no impediments.

The black dogs that followed were swifter,
their barking ancient, despicable.

As he fell, his chest turned to breastplate,
his one powerful arm covered with pagan signs.

Nearly stupid in my waiting for what would happen next,
each breath propelling me and him toward dust,
I woke, the sheets soaked, heart fluttering—:

When death comes into the sleeping room as through a tiny hole,
like a rent in the Covenant, it hurts.

SONGS FOR TWO SEASONS

Marsyas's Art

When the god came with his lute and knife,
asking, Have you made your last song?—

I told him I would make him the song for death:
great light of light, air like juice edging

around a figure torn into small tents, circles,
knitted chain, gold. And the scorning flute.

Procedure

The flesh comes free and the nodes
are loosened from their element.
The nerve will never stir; no
caress again will cause a tingle.

Bandages pack the numb chest,
the eyes are only half
opening—half wakened by the ebb
of drug tide.

Am I Gorgon, odd-
breasted, corrupt? I wonder. Bitter
complicity: the male nurse
nods and turns from me.

After Grave Illness

The body has two seasons
and doesn't exist to be changed;
it itself changes—as a clearing fills
with moths, then into it steps the hunted deer.
Who knows from the outside
where death grows?

I rub my eyes as if to recover
some first sight. Clouds purple.
There is rain; there's snow;
a northerly wind crushing in its teeth
the year's seeds.
I am pushed inside
out like a glove showing its lining.
Things simply are.

Red Pond

How cool it lies. It only speaks
of having little feeling—or too much.
Drop by scarlet drop its rhetoric spreads

to the farthest shore, waters
dislodging the pebbles and roots. Who watches?
Who watches this ancient mirror loves
the wind's effacement and the querulous silence,

water because of the sun,
sun because of drifting stars,
stars because of the beautiful surface
and traces of red mud.

ROBINSON CRUSOE'S HAIR

Poor Robin Crusoe, where are you? Where have you been? How came you here?

Poll

The lime tree, the eternal bars and bolts of the sea;
the marl cave; his compasses and books of navigation,

perspectives, dials; the great heats and no breeze;
the dog who could not talk to him; the parrot who sat on his finger

and laid his bill close to his face and did; barley; goatskin parasol;
three good Bibles; the principles of Nature;

the last uses of his ink to minute down the days
when strange things happened; the broken and imperfect prayers;

and when he was ill with fever, his hair—
chestnut like his father's—falling out, then growing back;

he felt the soft stubble at the temples;
he read Scriptures, hunted, preserved or cooked his kill, napped, built hedges,

and this gave him sometimes such covert joy; he rubbed
his fingertips lightly above his ears and behind where the two cords

of the neck run, and he could feel the hair multiply,
and it came in silvered and very curly, coarse almost

as the hair of coconuts:—All this balanced
against an earlier hardened despairing of dangers, and

once, as he rubbed back the new head of hair
in a torpor of distraction, the silent ceiling over silent sand,

he felt water squeeze from under his lids. And later when Friday stroked
his own father's face, fed him cakes, and chafed his arms and legs, he cried again.

THE ST. LOUIS ZOO

The isle is full of noises,
Sounds and sweet airs . . . sometimes voices.

The Tempest

High, yellow, coiled, and weighting the branch like an odd piece of fruit, a snake slept
by the gate, in the serpent house. I walked around the paths hearing

hushed air, piecemeal remarks, and the hoarse voice of the keeper spreading cabbage
and pellets in the elephant compound—"Hungry, are you? There's a girl.

How's Pearl?"—A clucking music, then silence again crept past me
on the waters of the duck pond. Birds with saffron wings in the flight cage

and flamingos the color of mangoes, even their webbed feet red-orange, made so
"by the algae they ingest," as angels are made of air—some bickered,

some were tongue-tied, some danced on one leg in the honeyed light.
I thought of autumn as leaves scattered down. Nearby, closed away

in his crude beginnings in a simulated rain forest, the gorilla pulled out handfuls
of grass, no Miranda to teach him to speak, though he was full of noises

and rank air after swallowing. Smooth rind and bearded husks lay about him.
His eyes were ingots when he looked at me.

In late summer air thick with rose and lily, I felt the old malevolence;
the snake tonguing the air, as if to tell me of its dreaming:—birds of paradise

gemming a pond; the unspooling; soft comings on, soft, soft
gestures, twisted and surreptitious; the shock; the taste; the kingdom.

In something more than words, You are the snake, snake coils in you,
it said. Do you think anyone knows its own hunger as well as the snake?

Why am I not just someone alive? When did Spirit tear me
to see how void of blessing I was? The snake hesitated, tasting dusk's black
    honey,

to feel if it was still good. And through its swoon
it knew it. Leaf, lichen, the least refinements, and the perfection.

KOMODO

The flight of a white cockatoo from tamarind to tamarind
still in his mind's eye, one morning Baron von Biberegg lay down

like a streak of flowers in the dust. Lush mist, animal calls and birds sinking, the
    mind
breeding without moving—O sleep, O golden hive. Then a giant lizard

appeared. When? Within an hour. In modern times.
As out of a dream's monstrous whirlpooling,

the monitor with flaming, olfactory tongue probing the air,
consumed the baron—hands, ivory teeth and bones, skin and fabric—,

whose sap mounted in terror or disbelief, groaned, spilled, then sank into the
    ground,
the sun deranged in the fronds.

○—○—○—○—○—○—○

To be utterly missing, given over like drying rain,
so that at some point his wife had to give up grieving,

his companions searching the bamboo groves, *tanah panas*, the unplumbed,
hot, estranging forests, then placing the white cross

to mark their last glimpse of him and to tell themselves
he *had* been, his having died filling them like abundance . . .

—wasn't he already a part of the dragon, visible in the yellow eyelids,
septic teeth, clawed feet solid as the bottoms of brass table legs?

Sentinel, snare, spirit, devourer, relative of the ascending bird.

◇-◇-◇-◇-◇-◇-◇

And the Promethean feasting; the shaking of the fragile frame
through sunrise and day; the throbbings through nighttime.

No one there to see the mouth tremble or to hear his thoughts.
Soul winces—as though divinity *could* be drained from him.

Yet Prometheus, yet the risings and settings of the stars we know
to follow, yet all the instructive frenzy lives

leaf by leaf, step by step, in the brandishing moment
and in the way the mountains and the savannas are waiting—

as the mind waits, the startled little bees that leap below sense and unseen.
Also fragments of liver, spoiling in the air, propose defiance.

◇-◇-◇-◇-◇-◇-◇

And the ones who study the monitor lizard while deer lie
napping in the azyma bushes—the ones for whom Orpheus's music

carries little sting or sweetness as they watch, in bird cry and tambourine
of sunlight, the lizards tongue the white fecal pellets of their rivals and who hold

the tongue and lashing tail in their hands for measurement? For them
neither heart nor devil nor god figure; no perfidy in the reptile's ambush; no
    metaphor;

only viscera, anatomy, the echoing straits between Indonesian islands, isolation,
   and escape.
Lizards prowl, eat, and mate, trued by the tips of their tails.

They lie in the grass or in their holes, with head outside the mouth
of the burrow and eyes wide open, staring into the black surrounding forest.

If this is it, if they completely inhabit themselves, there are no morals
or excuses. None for the disemboweled, disembodied: goats, pigs, horses,
the blazing cockatoo, the pink, lightless, inner tissues of the baron.

RELACIÓN OF CABEZA DE VACA

Cabeza de Vaca was one of four survivors of the Spanish expedition to the
west coast of Florida. He walked to Mexico among the hostile tribes as slave
and shaman. Later he was named governor of Paraguay, serving until his
overthrow by rivals in 1544, when he was returned to Spain in shackles.

Island of Ill Will, Louisiana, 1528

In February with truffle briar root and fish all gone,
a few of us as slaves ferried through the black marshland
to the upper keys to hunt for hare and scarcer deer . . .
the Indians a race of giants, weeping when first
they found us thrown naked on their shore . . . our drowned
at sand's edge rolling in the water like restless sleepers . . .
They fed and carried us from fire to fire for the bells
and beads we gave them . . . I asked myself by what design
these dark-skinned men, with canes jiggling at mouth
and breast, were made to watch over us . . . then three winds
blew in from the gulf and there was nothing left to eat . . .
I remember the wild light in the eyes of the hungriest,
soldiers who ran off during winter's tide, when the channels
are lowest, a rushing current of water over black mud . . .
When I learned their babble, the natives told me of a midden
of gnawed bones, the bodies eaten limb by limb.
I record their names: Sierra, Diego Lopez, Corral, Palacios,
Gonzalo Ruiz, their burial in the belly of the last
to die . . . nobody to make over this starving one the sign
of the cross on forehead and dead lips, recite a Pater Noster,
and give thanks for God's will and His mercy . . . nobody left
to eat him and bury him. What man knows his own end?

◇─◇─◇─◇─◇─◇─◇

All I have done wrong,
and my body remains, made now of fish oil and maize,
roots, fish jaws, worms. Yet used up. Light-headed, I have strange dreams.
They visit me after a fortnight's fever, in the burning and cold of fields.
I sweat and dream: an Indian stands
before me as the sun rises and washes his limbs in the light,
then places at my peeling feet
the glistening hearts of 600 deer. What carnal god
am I, I must bless them and feed myself? Their will be done?

My will. I open my eyes, the damned roar
of the sea at night and, somewhere, bells. It gets on my nerves.
Fly by, spirits of night, I whisper.
This island reeks of fish oil and mud.
We use the mud against the flies the island breeds.
It's as if everything is here in the wrong quantities. The mind is changed.
The spider guarding the door of its house, it bristles with meaning.
Its infant jabs are angry as I am angry. I could eat it.
Now it won't look at me. Has my soul gone away? Am I not here to see?

Only Dorantes, hidalgo, brother, understands what I will have to do,
I think he will come with me when I leave here.
I say to him what gain with the explorer, me,
for those who died in the mangroves, galled by their armor,
living by stolen maize, what honor? What gold? He nods and weeps. Then
    mourning, we sing
across the waters of Louisiana: *Fonte frida, fonte frida,*
fonte frida y con amor. Already, I confess,
he has saved one of the Indians, spitting on him, as is their custom, and praying.
It isn't likely to have any divine end and the Church will call it a devilish art.

Yet are we to become toads for priests, too weak and swollen
to give thanks for morning, for a single morsel of food?

The tribe weeps for a month when a child dies, and the family starves.
Yet they all starve slowly and do not mind. The land is white and barren. The
    sea is
full of fish some months and barren others. The men can run a deer five days
    into its grave
but will eat nothing until the children eat. The girls are reviled.
They all starve. They weep. They starve. They dance.
And I am thin as a boy before his first communion.
When they dream of evil, they slay the evildoer.
I wince in evil. Its blossoms fall on my shoulders and over the sand where I
    kneel.
I see the cruel spread shadow black with saints.
I brace, but no blow comes. No rod and sundering. Laughter.
Its flames lick my sins, straiten me on.
I must suffer the days like a stain
with these men. Whither they go, I must to pick roots and oysters.
I toughen in spring's desert, in the light of light.

I dream of Jerez and then dream of a Moor, lithe and sexual as a panther, who
    walks with us
to the west. There are deaths, thirsts, mountainous reaches,
and a coppery people who do not shun the Mystery
though their failings and mine drag with us. Food little,
chastened, all to be done, I am rapt, whether it will save me or throw me down,
deserving nothing. God, I hope, flies nearer this kindly world.
I dream and dream this future, and this, and exile.
Tomorrow I will say I want to cure the ailing. If they think I can be a man of
    fits and magics,
I will let them, holding my heart against their eyes, and heaven's mercy—

◯-◯-◯-◯-◯-◯-◯

Mexico City, 1536

Fades the sunlight through the window and I think
I can hear birds fluttering to rest in the *fresnos.*
In the courtyard I have heard them saying, "Peace is difficult, a frown
passing over the face of the river in the moonlight . . ."

Once I walked with a crowd of other simple people who wished
to make me believe that I not one instant die but endure and endure
the hollows and offenses of the body.
I ate a handful of deer tallow a day
and when there was more food I gave it all away, as all was given to me.
In the villages the people piled robes of hides, melons, turquoise, everything
that I might want to have, and turned away in silence as if this silence
were also something rare that I might want.

If you listen to a hush long enough, it becomes the held breath of tomorrow.

I have lain along the Rio Grande
and walked into the mountains.
I have said, "Let us go west, always toward the sun,"
and the people have wept, saying, "There is no one before you and no food,
but we will come with you."

I have passed by way of Samalayuca and sipped from its sweet water pools,
I know the narrow valley of Yaqui to Guasavas, where the women wash with the
    root of the yucca.
And I have seen skeletons hung to trees by Spanish ropes.

                    I have thought of the Second Calvary
and later processions, faint in orange light,

30

moving slowly because even in the singular mind of a mob there are
     swervings:
someone stops to piss or to chastise a sleepy child,
someone steps on the back of someone else's shoe.

Not knowing why, not hearing who, a thin continuous dreaming
of how it will end, they arrive and then, even as it happens, they are already
     leaving.

The dead one says *hunh?* and tomorrow comes on.
These birds sing of it to each other and listen,
crying *kreeah* for the late breeze, for the feel of it.

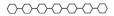

Madrid, 1546

When I was a slave, I spoke as a slave.
When I became governor, I spoke as governor. I am wronged in the charges.

          Answer the question.

Your Honors, the cow was slaughtered because my men were hungry. The
     Indian was paid.

          Did you order it?

Yes.

Yes, I forbade the Spanish from buying Guaranis slaves.
Yes, they ate them, even as the Spanish in Florida . . .

          Silence.

If I am guilty, I am guilty before God, not these inquisitors in black.
There is no metaphor for a man's pride and his hope, even as the bougainvilleas nod
their assent in the rain and sun, and the great palms look like young men in regalia.

Yes, I had a uniform made, but to wear for the Paititi of El Dorado when we
    found his city.
Yes, I used my seal, the head of a cow, like my father's and my father's father's,
but not in place of our Spanish king's.
Yes, I punished a hidalgo for striking an Indian chief, and I walked barefoot in
    the Paraguay nights.

There are only the signatures, seals, and attestations. Lies stare at them, fat and
    tender slaves,
and they smack their lips. They must hear me.

Was it for the sake of my health that chains were fastened around my ankles,
by my pillow a candle burned, no other light being admitted, and so damp that
    the grass grew
under my bed?—The red lumps of arsenic in my fish and meat, for my health's
    sake?

       Silence.

The fires? This scar on my brow?

       Silence!

Yes, I had Aracaré hanged.
Yes, I took girls from the friars and forbade our officials harems.
No! Never! I gave them to their fathers.
No, my acts were not of presumption and greed.
Yes, I slept outdoors when it was warm.

Even in prison I loved the nights in Asunción. The nights
were the longest nights I ever remember, and the stars were hidden with a tarp of trees.
A fragrance clung to the darkness, blue and violet like a youth's shut eyes. I could
    dream about
the stars and places and years, and the dreams mixed with my presence, with my body
shackled to a wooden post. Even now I am back in the Floridas,
and fifteen or twenty people are approaching me, unsure I am there; I weigh less than
    light.
I show one of them the tree crab in the palm of my hand.
How can anyone touch such things? one of them says, but another takes it from me to
    a mangrove
branch as if it were the most inviolate thing, as if understanding the style of the past.
Isn't clairvoyance a kind of style? The sound of the water which is no longer water but
    horses
frightened, and weak from many months on a ship? And voices flowering from a nail,
    a shell,
a mound of oyster shells where orange trees grow? . . .

    Guilty.

I dream and dream this future—
a turbulence—and this exile, a long sailing to a wild shore. The wind says hunh,
and the inlets of the mind change. Continuous. Continuous.

Cedar Key, 1993

Is it in a remembrance or a premonition of sunlight on sidewalk stones
and on the clean white shirt of a man on the steps to the library—
the down-driving light boiling over, as from an alchemist's flask,—
that I seem to return? I walk to the harbor restaurant, order a glass of port,

and watch a boat push out, rowing,
until with a great snap the sail fills. Several women at a near table look or maybe
look just past my forehead as I think (am I speaking?) about the distance that
   exists beyond
known lands: First, imagine that it doesn't. Then imagine

green domes and white sands inside a golden vacancy. The knuckles of the sailors
   roughen,
and they cast out of their hearts again and again such a place.
Only (I can tell them) in the last afternoon
will it rise up and gaze on them.

III

VOYAGE TO
BLACK POINT

Midway on our life's journey, I found myself
In dark woods, the right road lost.

Dante, *Inferno*

For I would travel without wind or sail,
And so, to lift sorrows from my mind,
Let your memories of sea days long fled
Pass over my spirit like an outspread sail.

What have you seen?

"We have seen lost sea beaches
And waves and stars and known many wars."

Charles Baudelaire, "Le Voyage"

. . . and once more saw the stars.

Dante, *Inferno*

BLACK POINT

I want to say oracle: sea grass: crab cluck:

swollen sheepshead in a fitful sea nodding assent::

I who listened for decades to familiar voicings

now heard Delphic imaginings low and sweet:

hallucinogenic as when the dolphin crests

in early morning vapor and light mixing on water

the leap and splash thunderous: a flight of birds:

one piping: syrinx in the wind: a rising sea—

woman behind the bank of ice who says

no crabs today: hours in a small boat

I converse with sea meadows

fish human nature: look and remember::

the zigzag to Black Point: Corycian Cove:

with my questions: alone suddenly

in panic—luminous neck of a snake

become a turtle: black and white tattered fish—

then the sort of trance: beneath sense some

early rune: I've traveled to hear this sound.

THE POET'S BLACK DRUM

Come in the silent acting in a dream now wayfarer

come back from that deepest paradise

where all that haven't breath the breathless mouth

may summon: Tell us all about your journey fishing::

barbels: stony teeth in the throat: aching shoulders:

and what Florida locals call tailing (the drifting fleece)—

drum underneath the flutter—: fecund

with slender parasites: beauty's flesh::

tasting of waters you taste and you say light dyed.

BLUE CRAB

A rearing up: the pincers waved in air: By God you better let me be:

brine bubbled at the mouth: bent foam and current having laved the shell:

water shouldering: Saturnal: deranged in the wire trap—

an inverted funnel like a halved hourglass—: ten legs makeshift on land::

How far its life reaches in the argosy beneath the surface of the sea: what I

ask: when emotion wakens: *Calli:* beautiful; *nectes:* swimmer::

To tumble down layers of sense into the warring gardens:

only to eat to molt to procreate: salt sea mud breeding in the shoals.

And then to come back, as from a museum: Goya barely bearable:

or from Medea's grave mind:: a taste of salt air:: I take up the crab in tongs.

SANDPIPER

Pillar of salt then the spell reversed: vowels

moistened in the mouth: tone of hurry::

in the distance weird bubbling whistle

bububu-hLeeyooo: Febru Febr-uary ooo:

how it is to be that happy and afraid:

now here alone rocking on the winter wave

hull dead bumping the shoal: wrists cold:

casting reeling in mind cold nothing not

for days: palm roots hold more movement:

until like Eurydice's head and shoulders come

into view something stirs water pearls on the line

fish nudging: I could weep for joy.

DOLPHIN

A slow storm coming across the gulf:

a raddling: wind in palmettos or a gaunt bird's bill?

Given ears and skin and eyes nose and tongue: given stories

of arrival—the perfect birth, Alexander's tide, Caesar's—

oh yearn fear portend contrive praise deny but not abstract::

I've seen the reddened knees of students in winter

in shorts when there was merely a slant of cold sun

and once tentacle burns across the chest of a dead tourist—

how blue the sea is, box jellyfish too few and small

*to matter. Neurotoxins, pfff. I'm . . .—*Well::

On leeward mangrove branches herons egrets:

yellow tridents rumbling far far away: on the horizon

a small bulge like the back of the giant

Hermes dolphin salt sparkling dark come bearing::

DROWNED

Open casket: a question of how they look: did look:——

salt lining in white rubber boots and pockets: wrapped in seine:

gunwale-bruised slightly on the forehead: still listening to what

the wind must have said: lashed by raiments

of rain: giving a last promise in return for everything still to come::

brine heaven: crabs who eat fish fish who eat crabs:

kingfish: mako: hardheaded catfish: ravenous ibises curving above:

land-buried without body: anchored: anchored:

yet still swimming in a hellish bright inlet:

seaweed in the beard: Odysseus too young for Troy:: so dreamed.

EDDY

Against wind's silk direction the tide is flowing,

turning on itself in the lee of salt marsh islands,

spiraling in large and little flowers that empetal

all below. The boat spins slowly and . . .

there'll come a change: yellowtail pulling on the line,

a closing of darkness: but, oh, in nature's matrix

for a few hours you lean neither away

nor toward . . . Whatever it is you refuse it.

EGRET

Violent leaner: fallen earthward: unconscious

of body left by soul: I am moved by its marble pose

above winter water brown and frothed:

the tiny fish like stars on a cloudy night:

stars stars stars in water at its feet:

it makes its bleak adjustments and waits:

yellow bill held en garde: wind swirling

lashing: if only it could tell: how tides

must move through it: one fish never enough.

LOW TIDE

Leave leave me on a naked island

mud and encrustations of oysters glittering

where through some magic I may forget

the always passing of day and night

hands canceling hands on the clock face

of a lover parent friend:: already now

the gulf's gray waters tick against the grass

gulls laugh and cry above my stranded hull

will start to rock the channel river flow like Acheron::

But for a spell wasn't there quiet winter tide

lowest nothing beckoning—no passage at all?

MANATEE

Shading to pink on the underparts: soft and liable

to be mistaken for Sirens: how sea sound comes

along the shore:: alone I found one shark-bitten deep

in the pelvic muscle floating near a shoal: water almost calm

light twinkling on oysters: fluting sweet shrill

fleur-de-lis: the western baths of early evening: clouds::

how we're saved from beauty beauty wanting

no other beauty but one:: with manatee in mind:—

gelid eye paddle-tail bloat—: my torn life myself surgeon-bitten::

my revocation:: in the mouth a pale root a word:

maculate flesh goldening as in a myth:: no more pretty songs.

MAN SO BRONZED

Forearms bulging lifting the giant cobia:

Xanthos River flowing from the west horizon:

wind subsiding, disintegrating, coming up::

maker of the gutted glistening fish

and maker of the evening: cold torrent in the eyes,

insolent ease in torso and hips: legendary

fish laid on the planks: burning river sinking

underneath the bay, darkness rocking, rippling—

you can hear it by the dock and feel the long day's motion

of the waves: a sort of dreaminess: the islanders

washing phosphorus from boats and gear:

sunset closing the marina. Hephaestus murmuring:—

the quality of cobia: steel gone from sinew

smithy cool: then gone to supper.

REDFISH

Loaves and fish: coelacanth: Bishop's jewfish:

the great silver fish that appeared to barter

life for three wishes: *tiburón:* eshark: puffer:

shark sucker: hammerhead: gag: in the riven waves

and rocking revery of Florida sun they feed on grass

and each other: my trailing bait: sweet smell of shrimp on fingers:

surface of water enameled: all all true——: the art and hell of it::

keep ammonia for catfish spines: loose the eye

or pluck it out: the lying on the side in water wiggle and flash

like resurrection——:: I'll tell you: north wind blew a recent morning

like acetylene: mud shone so and was freezing:

hands and feet burned with it: then the line swam upstream:

I came home marked with mud scales and fish slime:

mind in its parts admired the fight and iridescence

and remembered where to put the point of the knife:

blood swirled down the drain in the rinsing: I was happy::

What are living and dying if not the most natural

of ceremonies if practiced: not turned away from: not denied?

TO FISHERMEN

No more savage art: filleting: a deft pressure along the backbone

from tail fan to the red gills: fighting mystery with a honed blade

through the small bones: salt and scales on face and hands:: the Greek god,

as well, found flesh unmysterious, but in anger and disappointment:—

seagull cries, your music, are all about you: Apollonian but hungrier: nature is
   hungry::

the brave fish dies the birds swoop for the insides in no lovelier spirals.

SEA HARE

Gelatinous parching creature by the verge of the sea:

thick as a shoe: head dark green: sea a mixture of black

green blue: sky haunted by light rent with cries:

pelicans calling swimming in air folding wings

to dive into the sea: Bosch angels

changing shape as they're pursued from immaculate skies:

those few that accept the hideous and monstrous: fallen

a nightmare fauna—:: say the sea's to be questioned:

below the bounds of this estate though rainbowed cold

the rock-headed and cored of bone: chimera

our madness does not cease to reinvent which we dare not

think alive crawl in a thick ooze:: Yet even this one: torn

to the plain insides leaking dyes: exudes a gentle unrest of the soul::

Is it not good:: sea undulates: sharpening and smoothing

all the grooves history's graven in sand:: will you put hands

under the terrible flesh and heave it back to salt waters:

mirror of a lost estate: dawn time of the world's first season.

PELICAN

Rendings grunts after so much quiet: look:

tide is advancing—billows, mullet leaping toward shore:

also pigfish pinfish herring sheepshead silverside grass and top

minnows prawns:: brown pelicans—Audubon drawn

chestnut crosshatch iris blue rim reddened yellow tuft:

pistol-shot from wharves: beautiful evolutions

above the leaping shoal:: shot after shot::

made gumbo: salted: smoked: sensible to cold::

muting so profusely not a spot of green's left on the glossy mangrove::

esophagus storing fish: air pockets to cushion the blow:

black banners the drying wings after what is left

of watermire: wearing it: sitting in plainest light.

CLAM

What the sea does and what the sea does

for Mollusca: living in the gills of fish:: secreted a stony coat::

formed siphons anus stomach gills aorta foot::

the red tides come and go: salinities bacteria

boats storms:: compelling the imagination—Tarzan

in Coyuca Lagoon: giant lips around an ankle:

slitting the muscles and kicking free after breath's gone::

named cherrystone littleneck quahog *Moby*'s Queequeg.

Now the water's sixty degrees and a fisherman

with Giacometti forehead seeds mesh bags

fish gone deep into channels and rivers shine cold::

not for its brilliant anatomy nor just for the money

does he work so in this America:—malls where thousands

of sweet meat pounds are bought—: not for the generations

drowning by drowning:: being alone sun and wind

in his face he said harvesting.

ORCHID

In light's white rum in the light of the mind

bees come to the fertile stigmas

where with moderate degrees of force Darwin tested

Orchideae: the "wildest caprice"—

meaning cross-pollination: meaning their sensitivity

to pencil needles camel-hair brushes and his fingers::

Some wild orchids sicken by self-pollination::

others take on shapes so insects may alight thrashing calyx:

or resemble a pollinator's mate: smell luscious rotten::

so life spreads borne on a zephyr's back:: spreads

outside my window under the gold surface of water:

poured ointment of fishparts: dazing: whirling

through chambers of Byzantium:: mind's handiwork.

BOAT

Miscalculation the day's first high

from the last moon gulf Hades dark:

at 3 A.M. shrimp boat run aground

and engine grinding who else awake:

window so silver it seemed not light

nor any natural element:

again and again a throttling up

spewing water propeller scoring

the mud until tide lifted the keel:

one might have thought it was the engine—

however it was the hull began

to move offshore the window blackened

I stood until all throbbing sound

was blotted out absorbed by the dark

interstellar caves near the horizon

turned to clouds in the stir of morning::

low tide revealed the diagonal

across a glassy flat mimic of

a comet tail following greater light—:

heaven and hell have no memory

nor message nor direction beyond

this human mark fast disappearing.

NORTH KEY

Blues browns sudden shallows tide possessing

our way to the farthest key: narrow outlet where someone

left white markers past which we weren't to go:

overturned hull biting salt and burning sun: temple

mounds in a time the apostle Paul was writing

to Galatians: how can we not go on::

once we ran aground and were lifted

at daybreak: phoenix waters gray-red:—

once I only raised the motor and poled

to deeper water:: charts often wrong: storm

shift: cuts narrowed:: still fathoming the tides,

which seem not to change at all, not powerfully,

until all the basin shows and the sea's drenched

sound stops or starts anew: and sweet musk

of orchids is it? on a lunar breeze::

thus our reverie for the farthest isle

continues and on the shoulders of wind terrors

glide we fly past rivers to enter the other world:

our faint footsteps on the marsh's mud rim.

And then, then what, what more?

SNAKE KEY

Our sense of origin ourselves bedeviled:

Apollo Saturn: in the rose black garden Eve::

loving: killing:: labyrinthine the journey::

can't myth be left behind::

how it would be to start midkingdom::

standing by river water in marshes

never colored by another's eyes: saurian ripple:

flashing lances and silver spray of sunshine

through cat's claw palmetto: flung paths to the coast::

Muir describes two Negroes in firelight as devils:

they give him johnnycake: dire music

of the ibis he recalls: there are malarias:: wind

still fevers the tide: a small skiff lifts over the bar

to the outermost key: you can draw lime trees:

you can collect sea-worn shells:

you can count the snakes: you can:

but there's no way only back where you were::

SHORE

Go out alone against the tidal river which does not care for you:—

what or who could care in the end more than you—:

fin and tail leave no trails and darkness simply comes and goes:

an orange moon mirrored in dead calm moves only along

not with you and all creation belongs to itself::

the thought will calm you and your return if you return:—say

if you hear thunder or pretty lights reach from shore

as far as you have gone—: you can ride the last fertile waters

inland:: who then will better know life like a rind

bobbing on the tide and who better know to speak of it?

VOYAGE

Dantesque: staircase of birds descending: fish sparking

from the wet pyre: light that makes you feel day will never end::

I love and fear winding in these waters: deep corridors:

currents: shoals: iridescence boiling

suddenly: the back of something larger than my boat:

struck by light:: does the heart not darken: sins

sorrows winters:: but here coastal light—stellar

and enamel—isn't it the light—changes everything::

more than voyage:: with the great egret in slow glide

and manta ray—lion-colored: tail like Geryon—: by shell mounds

of the dead: wild marshes: wind rising: across

rugged gulf water: three rivers from cedar woods::

dark come evening and the crackle of stars!

IV

OLD PAN

LATE

Those perishing gentians splashed by moonlight and wind

as if to wash from dooryard and window a realization: later

a sort of cry and quick warbling bluhbluhbluhbluhbluhbluhbluh

down the scale a species and a field away

in June cross-dressing trees car parts and frames by the old farms

and the moist light:: even distrusting nature the light with beeswax

polished compounded light makes an aching

for the half-lived unread unloved syllables of moment and place

in my too sullen and meager heart I was above.

OLD PAN

1

Soft bleating Pan plays in the glade
where bees have taken over late
branches, swelling like fruit
sweeter for the lateness.

2

The reed and breathless voice
fans the bees when their ire
flies and lulls them to sleep
in one fertile body.

3

In charitable sunlight, high notes;
for the brown flanks of hills, laughter,
more laughter; as he runs there;
evenings the falling trills of doves.

4

It will be winter soon, too soon,
Pan will be rapt, still in snow,
but only a few will brave
the cold, and briefly.

5

Some cold nights in the woods
eyes half shut, remembering,
Pan dances while he plays,
to keep warm or just to dance!

6

Is it too much to speak of arpeggios
blood sugar and bees cascading,
with music so simple,
so nearly gone away?

$\diamond\!\!-\!\!\diamond\!\!-\!\!\diamond\!\!-\!\!\diamond\!\!-\!\!\diamond\!\!-\!\!\diamond$ NOTES

RELACIÓN OF CABEZA DE VACA

Island of Ill Will, Louisiana, 1528: After landing in Tampa Bay on April 15, 1528, three hundred Spanish explorers sailed and marched in several small groups up the gulf coast of wild Florida to the panhandle. Drownings, arrow wounds, disease, and increasing cold had diminished the number in de Vaca's party. Hunger was by far the worst difficulty, and on the island they named Malhado, five of the Christian sailors resorted to cannibalism.

Living with the Han and Capoque tribes, de Vaca was by turns a slave, a merchant to inland tribes, and a medicine man. His early medicine consisted of reciting the paternoster and Ave Maria, but during his long journey to Mexico, he practiced simple surgery, and he applied Indian cures—not without a guilty heart. His fame as a shaman grew, and in one Piman city in the Indies, he was presented with six hundred opened deer hearts.

Castillo was one of the three of de Vaca's companions who survived the journey to Mexico City: the others were Estevánico and Dorantes.

Mexico City, 1536: Nearing Mexico City, de Vaca saw the hanged bodies of Pima Indians and learned of the Spanish slave raids into Indian territory.

Madrid, 1546: De Vaca's trial before the Council of the Indies concerned his governorship of the Río de la Plata colony in Paraguay. His accusers were Spaniards who resented the list of edicts he had issued in 1542, which, among other things, forbade the enslavement and exploitation of native women.

He also forbade cannibalism among native tribes along the Paraguay River and fought Indian aggressors. Aracaré was the native guide of an exploratory expedition sent by de Vaca up the Paraguay River; after Aracaré's betrayal of the expedition, de Vaca had him hanged.

As in Mexico City after his long journey around the American gulf coast, de Vaca preferred to go barefoot and to sleep outdoors.

He was found guilty.

Cedar Key, 1993: Cabeza de Vaca's early expedition to Florida took him through or past Cedar Key.

BLACK POINT

lines 4–5: The narcotic gases rising from a nearby spring and preserved within the oracle's temple; Apollo once took form as a dolphin to swim out to sea and capture a group of sailors, whom he appointed the first priests of his cult in Delphi.

line 8: The reed pipe Pan made from the transformed body of the nymph Syrinx.

line 13: In mythology, the Corycian Cave, near Delphi and sacred to Pan.

line 15: The python slain by Apollo.

lines 17–18: Pan's and Apollo's music.

THE POET'S BLACK DRUM

lines 1–2: An invocation to an unnamed dead poet: Virgil perhaps or in modern times Elizabeth Bishop, who fished in Florida waters.

line 5: Barbels on the underjaw of black drums, which also have teeth down their gullets.

line 6: Drums fan their tails back and forth to keep in position while preying on small blue crabs hiding in oyster beds.

BLUE CRAB

line 3: Saturn devoured his sons.

line 9: Goya's painting of Saturn in the Prado.

DOLPHIN

line 4: Alexander is one of the "tyrants given to blood and plunder" (Pinsky, *The Inferno of Dante* [22.98]).

lines 8–10: The Coral Sea in summer is infested with box jellyfish, whose tentacles contain neurotoxins. The warning signs on northern Queensland beaches in Australia are sometimes ignored by tourists. The wounds gall the bare skin, are excruciating, and can kill.

DROWNED

line 2: Fishermen in Cedar Key wear white rubber boots; although commercial net fishing was stopped in 1994, the fishermen still throw nets.
line 10: Odysseus before he embarked for Troy and took his ten-year homeward journey.

EGRET

lines 1–6: The egret, fallen to earth, cannot see the fish below the water's surface; they are like the stars it cannot see now because of its obsessive gazing down. One of the three men who link their bodies in a wheel says to Dante, "If you escape from this dark sphere / To see the beauty of the stars, and relish / The pleasure then of saying, 'I was there'— / Speak word of us to others" (Pinsky, *The Inferno of Dante* [16.72–75]).

LOW TIDE

line 9: The river between the dark woods and hell's first circle.

MANATEE

line 1: Sirens for their music; falsifiers.
lines 3–11: References to some of the violent sins ("Across the Phlegethon River to the Plain of Fire [7th Circle]," in Pinsky, *The Inferno of Dante*).

MAN SO BRONZED

line 5: Hephaestus, a "maker," so an artist.
line 7: Both the Phlegethon and Xanthos rivers.

REDFISH

line 1: Elizabeth Bishop told Robert Lowell that the fish in "The Fish" was a jew-fish.

line 3: As noted in the last chapter of *The Old Man and the Sea.*

line 8: Ammonia and meat tenderizer are Florida remedies for catfish wounds, which are very painful.

SEA HARE

line 7: The hideous monsters in hell's depths: Geryon, the harpies, and sinners—"our human image so grotesquely reshaped" (Pinsky, *The Inferno of Dante* [20.22]).

CLAM

lines 5–6: Coyuca Lagoon, Pie de la Cuesta, Mexico, is where water shots for the 1950s television series with Johnny Weissmuller were filmed.

NORTH KEY

line 5: Timucuan shell mounds.

SNAKE KEY

lines 10–11: As told in chapter 5 of John Muir's *A Thousand-Mile Walk to the Gulf.*

VOYAGE

line 10: Geryon in *Inferno,* whose tail is quivery and restless with a venomous point.

line 12: The Acheron, Styx, and Phlegethon in *Inferno;* Channel 6, Goose Creek, and Sand Creek between Cedar Key and Black Point.

line 13: E quindi uscimmo a riveder le stelle (34.140).

⬡-⬡-⬡-⬡-⬡-⬡ ABOUT THE AUTHOR

Carol Frost divides her time between Cedar Key, Florida, and upstate New York. Her most recent collections of poetry are *I Will Say Beauty* and *Love and Scorn: New and Selected Poems,* also published by TriQuarterly Books/Northwestern University Press. Among her many honors and prizes are three Pushcart Prize anthology appearances and two fellowships from the National Endowment for the Arts. She has taught at Washington University in St. Louis and as poet in residence at the Stadler Center for Poetry at Bucknell University. A professor of English and writer in residence at Hartwick College, she also directs the Catskill Poetry Workshop.